THE SUPREME

DALLAS MAVERICKS

TRIVIA AND QUIZBOOK

BY: JACKSON WELLS

Table of Contents

INTRODUCTION TO DALLAS MAVERICKS

The St. Louis Cardinals, an institution steeped in baseball tradition and adorned with a legacy of excellence, proudly stand as one of the most revered franchises in Major League Baseball. Since their founding in 1882, the Cardinals have woven an intricate tapestry of success, claiming an impressive number of World Series championships and etching their name into the annals of baseball history. Nestled on the banks of the Mississippi River, the Cardinals have become synonymous with Midwestern grit, embodying the essence of a team deeply rooted in community and fervently supported by the passionate Redbird Nation. With a commitment to fostering talent, sportsmanship, and a relentless pursuit of victory, the St. Louis Cardinals command respect not only for their on-field prowess but also for their enduring impact on the hearts of baseball enthusiasts across the nation. This is the story of a franchise that transcends generations, where the iconic Cardinal red represents not just a team, but a timeless symbol of baseball excellence.

TEAM HISTORY
QUESTION TIME!

1. When were the Dallas Mavericks founded?

   a. 1978

   b. 1980

   c. 1985

   d. 1990

2. What is the team's nickname?

   a. Mavericks

   b. Mustangs

   c. Stallions

   d. Texans

3. In which conference do the Mavericks compete?

   a. Eastern Conference

   b. Western Conference

   c. Central Conference

   d. Southern Conference

4. Who is the owner of the Dallas Mavericks?

   a. Mark Cuban

b. Jerry Jones

c. Michael Jordan

d. Magic Johnson

5. In which year did the Mavericks make their first NBA playoff appearance?

a. 1984

b. 1986

c. 1990

d. 1994

6. Who is the all-time leading scorer for the Dallas Mavericks?

a. Dirk Nowitzki

b. Jason Kidd

c. Rolando Blackman

d. Michael Finley

7. How many NBA championships have the Mavericks won as of 2022?

a. 1

b. 2

c. 3

d. 0

8. What color are the Mavericks' home jerseys?

   a. Blue

   b. Green

   c. White

   d. Black

9. Which arena do the Mavericks call their home?

   a. Staples Center

   b. American Airlines Center

   c. Madison Square Garden

   d. Oracle Arena

10. Who was the first head coach of the Dallas Mavericks?

   a. Dick Motta

   b. Don Nelson

   c. Avery Johnson

   d. Rick Carlisle

11. In which year did the Mavericks win their first NBA championship?

   a. 2006

   b. 2011

c. 2008

d. 2015

12. What was the Mavericks' record for most wins in a single regular season?

a. 60

b. 67

c. 55

d. 50

13. Which player won the NBA Finals MVP in the Mavericks' championship-winning year?

a. Dirk Nowitzki

b. Jason Terry

c. Shawn Marion

d. Tyson Chandler

14. How many retired numbers does the Dallas Mavericks franchise have (as of 2022)?

a. 1

b. 3

c. 5

d. 7

15. Who is known as the "Mavs Man" and serves as the team's mascot?

  a. Maverick the Horse

  b. Mavrick the Maverick

  c. Dirk the Dunking Dino

  d. None of the above

16. Which team is considered the primary rival of the Dallas Mavericks?

  a. Houston Rockets

  b. San Antonio Spurs

  c. Los Angeles Lakers

  d. Oklahoma City Thunder

17. What is the Mavericks' longest winning streak in franchise history?

  a. 12 games

  b. 17 games

  c. 22 games

  d. 27 games

18. Who holds the record for the most assists in a single game for the Mavericks?

a. Steve Nash

b. Jason Kidd

c. Derek Harper

d. Rajon Rondo

19. How many times have the Mavericks hosted the NBA All-Star Game?

    a. 1

    b. 2

    c. 3

    d. 4

20. Which player was selected as the first overall pick by the Mavericks in the NBA Draft?

    a. Dirk Nowitzki

    b. Jason Kidd

    c. Luka Dončić

    d. Jamal Mashburn

21. What is the Mavericks' team slogan?

    a. "Mavs Nation"

    b. "Dallas Pride"

    c. "MFFL" (Mavs Fan for Life)

d. "Lone Star Ballers"

22. Which coach led the Mavericks to their first NBA Finals appearance?

a. Rick Carlisle

b. Avery Johnson

c. Don Nelson

d. Dick Motta

23. Who is the Mavericks' all-time leader in three-pointers made?

a. Dirk Nowitzki

b. Jason Terry

c. Wesley Matthews

d. Michael Finley

24. Which city did the Mavericks represent before moving to Dallas?

a. Kansas City

b. Seattle

c. Vancouver

d. San Diego

25. Who holds the record for the most rebounds in a single game for the Mavericks?

a. Tyson Chandler

b. Dirk Nowitzki

c. Shawn Bradley

d. Roy Tarpley

26. What was the Mavericks' first-ever NBA Draft pick in 1980?

a. Rolando Blackman

b. Mark Aguirre

c. Derek Harper

d. Sam Perkins

27. How many times have the Mavericks won the Southwest Division title (as of 2022)?

a. 2

b. 4

c. 6

d. 8

28. Who is the youngest player to debut for the Mavericks in franchise history?

a. Luka Dončić

b. Dennis Smith Jr.

c. Josh Green

d. Dirk Nowitzki

29. What was the Mavericks' original team name before they officially became the Mavericks?

a. Dallas Texans

b. Texas Shooters

c. Dallas Stallions

d. Dallas Wranglers

30. In which year did the Mavericks retire Dirk Nowitzki's jersey number?

a. 2019

b. 2020

c. 2021

d. 2022

ANSWERS

1. a

2. a

3. b

4. a

5. b

6. a

7. a

8. a

9. b

10. b

11. b

12. b

13. a

14. c

15. a

16. b

17. c

18. b

19. b

20. a

21. c

22. b

23. b

24. a

25. a

26. c

27. c

28. b

29. c

30. c

CHAMPIONSHIP AND PLAYOFF RUNS
QUESTION TIME!

1. In which year did the Dallas Mavericks win their first NBA championship?

   a. 2006

   b. 2008

   c. 2010

   d. 2011

2. Who was the NBA Finals MVP when the Mavericks won their first championship?

   a. Dirk Nowitzki

   b. Jason Terry

   c. Shawn Marion

   d. Tyson Chandler

3. Which team did the Mavericks defeat in the NBA Finals to win their first championship?

   a. Miami Heat

   b. Los Angeles Lakers

   c. Boston Celtics

d. San Antonio Spurs

4. How many games did the Mavericks win in the NBA Finals during their championship year?

a. 4

b. 5

c. 6

d. 7

5. Who was the head coach of the Dallas Mavericks during their first championship run?

a. Rick Carlisle

b. Avery Johnson

c. Don Nelson

d. Dick Motta

6. What was the Mavericks' regular-season record in the year they won their first championship?

a. 60-22

b. 63-19

c. 55-27

d. 58-24

7. How many NBA Finals appearances have the Mavericks made in total (as of 2022)?

    a. 2

    b. 3

    c. 4

    d. 5

8. In which year did the Mavericks make their first-ever NBA playoff appearance?

    a. 1984

    b. 1986

    c. 1988

    d. 1990

9. How many NBA Finals games did the Mavericks lose before winning their first championship?

    a. 1

    b. 2

    c. 3

    d. 4

10. Which team did the Mavericks face in the Western Conference Finals during their championship year?

    a. Los Angeles Lakers

b. Oklahoma City Thunder

c. San Antonio Spurs

d. Golden State Warriors

11. Who hit the game-winning three-pointer in Game 2 of the 2011 NBA Finals?

a. Dirk Nowitzki

b. Jason Kidd

c. Jason Terry

d. Shawn Marion

12. How many times have the Mavericks been eliminated in the first round of the NBA playoffs (as of 2022)?

a. 6

b. 8

c. 10

d. 12

13. In the 2006 NBA Finals, the Mavericks lost to which team?

a. Miami Heat

b. San Antonio Spurs

c. Detroit Pistons

d. Los Angeles Lakers

14. Who is the all-time leading scorer for the Mavericks in NBA playoff history?

a. Dirk Nowitzki

b. Jason Terry

c. Rolando Blackman

d. Michael Finley

15. How many times have the Mavericks reached the NBA Finals without winning the championship?

a. 1

b. 2

c. 3

d. 4

16. Who was the head coach of the Mavericks when they made their first NBA Finals appearance?

a. Rick Carlisle

b. Avery Johnson

c. Don Nelson

d. Dick Motta

17. Which team did the Mavericks defeat in the 2011 Western Conference Finals to advance to the NBA Finals?

a. San Antonio Spurs

b. Oklahoma City Thunder

c. Los Angeles Lakers

d. Golden State Warriors

18. In the 2003 NBA Playoffs, the Mavericks reached the Western Conference Finals but lost to which team?

a. San Antonio Spurs

b. Los Angeles Lakers

c. Sacramento Kings

d. Minnesota Timberwolves

19. How many games did the Mavericks win in the 2006 NBA Finals against the Miami Heat?

a. 2

b. 3

c. 4

d. 5

20. Who is the Mavericks' all-time leader in three-pointers made in NBA playoff games?

a. Dirk Nowitzki

b. Jason Terry

c. Wesley Matthews

d. Michael Finley

21. In the 2011 NBA Finals, who led the Mavericks in scoring in the decisive Game 6?

    a. Dirk Nowitzki

    b. Jason Terry

    c. Shawn Marion

    d. Tyson Chandler

22. How many times have the Mavericks won the NBA Western Conference Championship (as of 2022)?

    a. 1

    b. 2

    c. 3

    d. 4

23. Which team did the Mavericks defeat in the 2006 Western Conference Finals to reach the NBA Finals?

    a. San Antonio Spurs

    b. Phoenix Suns

    c. Los Angeles Lakers

    d. Utah Jazz

24. Who was the Mavericks' opponent in the first round of the 2010 NBA Playoffs?

    a. San Antonio Spurs

    b. Portland Trail Blazers

    c. Houston Rockets

    d. Memphis Grizzlies

25. In the 2011 NBA Finals, the Mavericks won Game 5 on the road against which team?

    a. Miami Heat

    b. Chicago Bulls

    c. Boston Celtics

    d. Los Angeles Lakers

26. How many games did the Mavericks win in the 2003 NBA Finals?

    a. 1

    b. 2

    c. 3

    d. 4

27. Which Mavericks player was named the NBA Finals MVP in the year they won their first championship?

a. Dirk Nowitzki

b. Jason Terry

c. Shawn Marion

d. Tyson Chandler

28. In the 2011 NBA Playoffs, the Mavericks defeated the Lakers in the second round, sweeping them in how many games?

a. 2

b. 3

c. 4

d. 5

29. How many NBA Finals MVP awards has Dirk Nowitzki won throughout his career?

a. 1

b. 2

c. 3

d. 0

30. Who was the coach of the Mavericks when they made their second NBA Finals appearance?

a. Rick Carlisle

b. Avery Johnson

c. Don Nelson

d. Dick Motta

ANSWERS

1. 2011

2. Miami Heat

3. Dirk Nowitzki

4. Jason Terry

5. 15

6. Steve Nash

7. 2006

8. Michael Finley

9. Jason Kidd

10. 2007

11. San Antonio Spurs

12. NBA Finals MVP

13. 2005-2006

14. Western Conference Finals

15. Tyson Chandler

16. 3

17. 1980-1981

18. Houston Rockets

19. Sacramento Kings

20. 2015-2016

21. Shawn Marion

22. Denver Nuggets

23. 50-32

24. 2019-2020

25. 3

26. Golden State Warriors

27. 1990-1991

28. Rolando Blackman

29. 2010

30. 1997

KEY PLAYERS
QUESTION TIME!

1. Who is the all-time leading scorer for the Dallas Mavericks?

   a. Jason Kidd

   b. Dirk Nowitzki

   c. Michael Finley

   d. Rolando Blackman

2. Which player is known as "The Jet" and played a key role in the Mavericks' championship run in 2011?

   a. Jason Kidd

   b. Jason Terry

   c. Shawn Marion

   d. Tyson Chandler

3. In which year did Dirk Nowitzki retire from professional basketball?

   a. 2018

   b. 2019

   c. 2020

   d. 2021

4. Which Mavericks player was known for his "Matrix" nickname due to his versatile playing style?

a. Dirk Nowitzki

b. Jason Kidd

c. Shawn Marion

d. Michael Finley

5. Who is the Mavericks' all-time leader in assists?

a. Jason Terry

b. Derek Harper

c. Jason Kidd

d. Steve Nash

6. Which player won the NBA Finals MVP in the Mavericks' championship year of 2011?

a. Jason Kidd

b. Jason Terry

c. Dirk Nowitzki

d. Tyson Chandler

7. What is the nationality of Dirk Nowitzki, one of the greatest players in Mavericks history?

a. American

b. German

c. Canadian

d. Spanish

8. Which Mavericks player is known for his iconic one-legged fadeaway shot?

a. Jason Kidd

b. Luka Dončić

c. Dirk Nowitzki

d. Kristaps Porziņģis

9. In which year did Luka Dončić make his NBA debut for the Dallas Mavericks?

a. 2017

b. 2018

c. 2019

d. 2020

10. Who was the first Mavericks player to have his jersey number retired?

a. Jason Kidd

b. Dirk Nowitzki

c. Rolando Blackman

d. Michael Finley

11. Which player is known for his nickname "The Unicorn" due to his unique skill set?

a. Kristaps Porziņģis

b. Tyson Chandler

c. Jason Terry

d. Steve Nash

12. Who is the Mavericks' all-time leader in three-pointers made?

a. Dirk Nowitzki

b. Jason Terry

c. Wesley Matthews

d. Michael Finley

13. Which player was known for his leadership on and off the court and played a key role in the Mavericks' 2011 championship?

a. Tyson Chandler

b. Jason Kidd

c. Shawn Marion

d. Vince Carter

14. What is the position of Dirk Nowitzki, who played 21 seasons with the Dallas Mavericks?

   a. Point Guard

   b. Shooting Guard

   c. Small Forward

   d. Power Forward

15. Who holds the record for the most points scored in a single game for the Dallas Mavericks?

   a. Dirk Nowitzki

   b. Jamal Mashburn

   c. Rolando Blackman

   d. Luka Dončić

16. Which player was selected by the Mavericks as the third overall pick in the 1994 NBA Draft?

   a. Michael Finley

   b. Jamal Mashburn

   c. Jason Kidd

   d. Jim Jackson

17. In which season did Jason Kidd win the NBA Rookie of the Year award with the Dallas Mavericks?

a. 1993-94

b. 1994-95

c. 1995-96

d. 1996-97

18. Who is known for his tenure as the Mavericks' "floor general" and later became the team's head coach?

a. Jason Kidd

b. Jason Terry

c. Derek Harper

d. Rick Carlisle

19. Which player was acquired by the Mavericks in a trade that involved sending Devin Harris to the New Jersey Nets?

a. Tyson Chandler

b. Jason Terry

c. Jason Kidd

d. Shawn Marion

20. Who was the first Mavericks player to be selected as an NBA All-Star?

a. Rolando Blackman

b. Mark Aguirre

c. Derek Harper

d. Brad Davis

21. Which player is known for his time with the Mavericks as a high-scoring shooting guard and small forward?

    a. Michael Finley

    b. Rolando Blackman

    c. Jamal Mashburn

    d. Jason Kidd

22. Who is the youngest player to record a triple-double in Mavericks history?

    a. Jason Kidd

    b. Luka Dončić

    c. Dennis Smith Jr.

    d. Jamal Mashburn

23. Which player was part of the Mavericks' "Big Three" alongside Dirk Nowitzki and Jason Terry during the 2010-2011 season?

    a. Tyson Chandler

    b. Shawn Marion

    c. Caron Butler

    d. Jason Kidd

24. What is the position of Jason Terry, who played a significant role in the Mavericks' championship run in 2011?

a. Point Guard

b. Shooting Guard

c. Small Forward

d. Power Forward

25. Who was the Mavericks' first-round draft pick in the 2018 NBA Draft?

a. Luka Dončić

b. Jalen Brunson

c. Dennis Smith Jr.

d. Justin Anderson

26. Which player is known for his defensive prowess and played a crucial role in the Mavericks' 2011 championship?

a. Tyson Chandler

b. Shawn Marion

c. DeShawn Stevenson

d. Brendan Haywood

27. Who is the Mavericks' all-time leader in steals?

a. Jason Kidd

b. Derek Harper

c. Michael Finley

d. Rolando Blackman

28. Which player was selected by the Mavericks as the fifth overall pick in the 2017 NBA Draft?

a. Dennis Smith Jr.

b. Luka Dončić

c. Jalen Brunson

d. Justin Anderson

29. In which year did the Mavericks retire Dirk Nowitzki's jersey number?

a. 2019

b. 2020

c. 2021

d. 2022

30. Which player holds the record for the most assists in a single game for the Dallas Mavericks?

a. Steve Nash

b. Jason Kidd

c. Derek Harper

d. Rajon Rondo

ANSWERS

1. Dirk Nowitzki

2. Jason Terry

3. 2019

4. Shawn Marion

5. Jason Kidd

6. Dirk Nowitzki

7. German

8. Dirk Nowitzki

9. 2018

10. Dirk Nowitzki

11. Kristaps Porziņģis

12. Dirk Nowitzki

13. Jason Kidd

14. Power Forward

15. Dirk Nowitzki

16. Jason Kidd

17. 1994-1995

18. Jason Kidd

19. Tyson Chandler

20. Rolando Blackman

21. Michael Finley

22. Luka Dončić

23. Caron Butler

24. Shooting Guard

25. Luka Dončić

26. Tyson Chandler

27. Jason Kidd

28. Luka Dončić

29. 2021

30. Jason Kidd

OWNER AND MANAGEMENT
QUESTION TIME!

1. Who is the current owner of the Dallas Mavericks?

  a. Mark Cuban

  b. Jerry Jones

  c. Michael Jordan

  d. Magic Johnson

2. In which year did Mark Cuban purchase the Dallas Mavericks?

  a. 1998

  b. 2000

  c. 2002

  d. 2004

3. What is Mark Cuban's primary business background before owning the Mavericks?

  a. Technology

  b. Real Estate

  c. Entertainment

  d. Finance

4. Who is the president of basketball operations and general manager of the Dallas Mavericks?

   a. Donnie Nelson

   b. Rick Carlisle

   c. Dirk Nowitzki

   d. Jason Kidd

5. In which year did Rick Carlisle become the head coach of the Dallas Mavericks?

   a. 2007

   b. 2009

   c. 2011

   d. 2013

6. Which former Mavericks player serves as a special advisor to the team's owner, Mark Cuban?

   a. Jason Kidd

   b. Dirk Nowitzki

   c. Michael Finley

   d. Rolando Blackman

7. Who is the CEO of the Dallas Mavericks and oversees the day-to-day operations of the franchise?

   a. Donnie Nelson

b. Rick Carlisle

c. Cynthia Marshall

d. Bob Voulgaris

8. What significant change did Cynthia Marshall implement after joining the Mavericks organization in 2018?

a. New team logo and colors

b. Overhaul of the coaching staff

c. Diversity and inclusion initiatives

d. Relocation of the team's home arena

9. Who is responsible for the Mavericks' player personnel decisions, including drafts and trades?

a. Rick Carlisle

b. Mark Cuban

c. Donnie Nelson

d. Cynthia Marshall

10. In which role did Donnie Nelson initially join the Dallas Mavericks organization?

a. Head Coach

b. General Manager

c. Team Physician

d. Marketing Director

11. Who was the head coach of the Mavericks when they won their first NBA championship in 2011?

a. Rick Carlisle

b. Avery Johnson

c. Don Nelson

d. Dick Motta

12. Which former NBA player and coach serves as the Mavericks' Vice President of Basketball Operations?

a. Jason Kidd

b. Michael Finley

c. Dirk Nowitzki

d. Derek Harper

13. In which year did the Dallas Mavericks officially hire their first female CEO?

a. 2017

b. 2018

c. 2019

d. 2020

14. Who is the Chief Technology Officer for the Dallas Mavericks and is known for his analytics expertise?

a. Donnie Nelson

b. Rick Carlisle

c. Mark Cuban

d. Bob Voulgaris

15. What is the role of the Mavericks' Chief Marketing Officer?

a. Player Development

b. Community Engagement

c. Branding and Promotion

d. Financial Management

16. Who serves as the Mavericks' Chief Financial Officer, overseeing the team's financial operations?

a. Cynthia Marshall

b. Donnie Nelson

c. Bob Voulgaris

d. J.J. Barea

17. Which former NBA player and Mavericks legend is involved in the team's front office as a consultant?

a. Jason Kidd

b. Dirk Nowitzki

c. Michael Finley

d. Rolando Blackman

18. Who holds the position of Chief Diversity, Equity, and Inclusion Officer for the Dallas Mavericks?

a. Donnie Nelson

b. Rick Carlisle

c. Cynthia Marshall

d. Mark Cuban

19. Which member of the Mavericks' management team is responsible for overseeing player development?

a. Jason Kidd

b. Dirk Nowitzki

c. Michael Finley

d. God Shammgod

20. Who is the Mavericks' Director of Scouting and is actively involved in the team's draft decisions?

a. Rick Carlisle

b. Donnie Nelson

c. Michael Finley

d. Bob Voulgaris

21. What is the name of the Mavericks' mascot, who is also involved in community outreach programs?

a. Mavs Man

b. Dunkin' Dino

c. Mavericks Max

d. Hoop Hound

22. Which member of the Mavericks' front office is responsible for overseeing sports science and player health?

a. Donnie Nelson

b. Casey Smith

c. Rick Carlisle

d. Cynthia Marshall

23. Who is the Mavericks' Director of Basketball Administration and Salary Cap expert?

a. Donnie Nelson

b. Bob Voulgaris

c. Michael Finley

d. Keith Grant

24. Which former NBA player serves as the Mavericks' Director of Player Development?

a. Jason Kidd

b. Dirk Nowitzki

c. Michael Finley

d. Rolando Blackman

25. In which year did the Dallas Mavericks celebrate their 40th anniversary, hosting special events and promotions?

a. 2018

b. 2019

c. 2020

d. 2021

26. Who is responsible for managing the Mavericks' public relations and communication strategies?

a. Rick Carlisle

b. Mark Cuban

c. Scott Tomlin

d. Derek Harper

27. Which former NBA player serves as the Mavericks' Director of Player Wellness?

a. Jason Kidd

b. God Shammgod

c. Michael Finley

d. Rolando Blackman

28. What is the role of the Mavericks' Director of Corporate Partnerships?

a. Community Outreach

b. Marketing and Branding

c. Business Development

d. Player Relations

29. Which member of the Mavericks' management team oversees the team's social media and digital content?

a. Mark Cuban

b. Michael Finley

c. Bob Voulgaris

d. Tony Ronzone

30. Who is responsible for managing the Mavericks' game operations and fan experience?

a. Dirk Nowitzki

b. Cynthia Marshall

c. Donnie Nelson

d. Roland Beech

ANSWERS

1. Mark Cuban

2. 2000

3. Entertainment

4. Donnie Nelson

5. 2008

6. Dirk Nowitzki

7. Cynthia Marshall

8. Diversity and inclusion initiatives

9. Donnie Nelson

10. General Manager

11. Rick Carlisle

12. Michael Finley

13. 2018

14. Bob Voulgaris

15. Branding and Promotion

16. Cynthia Marshall

17. Jason Kidd

18. 2020

19. Dennis Smith Jr.

20. Rolando Beech

21. Rick Carlisle

22. Casey Smith

23. Keith Grant

24. Jason Kidd

25. 2019

26. Scott Tomlin

27. God Shammgod

28. Derek Harper

29. Tony Ronzone

30. Roland Beech

RIVALRIES
QUESTION TIME!

1. Which team is considered the primary rival of the Dallas Mavericks?

   a. San Antonio Spurs

   b. Houston Rockets

   c. Memphis Grizzlies

   d. Los Angeles Lakers

2. What is the name of the trophy awarded to the winner of the regular-season series between the Mavericks and the Houston Rockets?

   a. Lone Star Trophy

   b. Texas Cup

   c. Alamo Cup

   d. Maverick Cup

3. In which season did the rivalry between the Mavericks and the Houston Rockets intensify, leading to the creation of a trophy?

   a. 1990-91

   b. 1996-97

   c. 2001-02

d. 2010-11

4. Which former player, known for his time with the Houston Rockets, played a key role in fueling the Mavericks-Rockets rivalry?

a. Hakeem Olajuwon

b. Tracy McGrady

c. Yao Ming

d. Clyde Drexler

5. What incident in 2005 heightened the rivalry between the Mavericks and the San Antonio Spurs?

a. Playoff brawl

b. Coaching feud

c. Blockbuster trade

d. Mascot altercation

6. In the 2006 NBA Playoffs, the Mavericks faced the Spurs in a memorable seven-game series. What was the outcome?

a. Mavericks won 4-3

b. Spurs won 4-3

c. Series tied 3-3

d. Series canceled

7. Which Spurs player is known for his battles with Dirk Nowitzki and is often considered a Mavericks antagonist?

a. Tim Duncan

b. Tony Parker

c. Manu Ginobili

d. Bruce Bowen

8. What is the name of the highway that connects Dallas and San Antonio, symbolizing the rivalry between the Mavericks and the Spurs?

a. I-10

b. I-20

c. I-35

d. I-45

9. Which team has a rivalry with the Mavericks known as the "I-35 Rivalry" due to the proximity of their respective cities?

a. San Antonio Spurs

b. Houston Rockets

c. Oklahoma City Thunder

d. New Orleans Pelicans

10. The Mavericks faced the Miami Heat in the NBA Finals in 2006 and 2011, creating a rivalry. Which player was a common factor in both matchups?

a. Dwyane Wade

b. LeBron James

c. Chris Bosh

d. Shaquille O'Neal

11. What was the result of the 2006 NBA Finals between the Mavericks and the Miami Heat?

a. Mavericks won

b. Heat won

c. Series tied

d. Finals canceled

12. Who hit the game-winning three-pointer in Game 2 of the 2011 NBA Finals against the Miami Heat?

a. Dirk Nowitzki

b. Jason Kidd

c. Jason Terry

d. Shawn Marion

13. The Mavericks had a playoff rivalry with the Oklahoma City Thunder. In which year did they face each other in the Western Conference Finals?

a. 2009

b. 2011

c. 2013

d. 2016

14. Who is known for his battles with Dirk Nowitzki and was a key figure in the Thunder's rivalry with the Mavericks?

a. Russell Westbrook

b. Kevin Durant

c. James Harden

d. Serge Ibaka

15. What is the nickname of the rivalry between the Dallas Mavericks and the Los Angeles Lakers?

a. Lone Star Showdown

b. Mavericks-Lakers Classic

c. Texas Tussle

d. Hollywood Hoopla

16. In the 1988 NBA Playoffs, the Mavericks faced the Lakers in the Western Conference Finals. What was the outcome of the series?

 a. Mavericks won

 b. Lakers won

 c. Series tied

 d. Finals canceled

17. Which Lakers player is known for his battles with the Mavericks, particularly during the 1980s?

 a. Magic Johnson

 b. Kareem Abdul-Jabbar

 c. James Worthy

 d. Michael Cooper

18. What is the nickname given to the Mavericks-Lakers rivalry due to the teams' high-scoring and entertaining matchups?

 a. Shootout Showdown

 b. Points Parade

 c. Offensive Extravaganza

 d. Showtime vs. Big D

19. The Mavericks faced the Sacramento Kings in a memorable playoff series in 2003. What was unique about this series?

a. It went to seven overtimes

b. It featured a quadruple-double performance

c. It was the first-ever playoff meeting between the teams

d. It included a game-winning half-court shot

20. In the 2011 NBA Playoffs, the Mavericks faced which team in the first round, creating a short-lived but intense rivalry?

a. Portland Trail Blazers

b. Denver Nuggets

c. Utah Jazz

d. New Orleans Hornets

21. The Mavericks have a regional rivalry with the New Orleans Pelicans. What is the name of this rivalry?

a. Battle of the South

b. Gulf Coast Clash

c. Pelican Prairie Duel

d. Texas-South Tussle

22. In which year did the Mavericks and the New York Knicks engage in a heated rivalry during the NBA Finals?

a. 1994

b. 1999

c. 2000

d. 2002

23. Who is known for his battles with Dirk Nowitzki and was a key player for the New York Knicks during their rivalry with the Mavericks?

a. Patrick Ewing

b. Allan Houston

c. Latrell Sprewell

d. Charles Oakley

24. Which team did the Mavericks face in the 2014 NBA Playoffs, creating a rivalry known as the "Texas Duel"?

a. Houston Rockets

b. San Antonio Spurs

c. Memphis Grizzlies

d. Golden State Warriors

25. The Mavericks have a historical rivalry with the Portland Trail Blazers. In which year did they face each other in the NBA Playoffs for the first time?

a. 1985

b. 1987

c. 1990

d. 1992

26. What is the name of the rivalry between the Dallas Mavericks and the Utah Jazz?

   a. Mountain Mavericks Melee

   b. Western Whirlwind

   c. Jazz Jump Ball

   d. High Plains Showdown

27. In the 2019-2020 NBA season, the Mavericks faced the Los Angeles Clippers in the playoffs, renewing a recent rivalry. What was unique about this matchup?

   a. It was the first playoff meeting between the teams

   b. The series went to seven overtimes

   c. Luka Dončić hit a game-winning buzzer-beater

   d. Both teams were undefeated in the regular season

28. The Mavericks faced the Golden State Warriors in the 2007 NBA Playoffs, marking the beginning of a rivalry. What was the outcome of that series?

   a. Mavericks won

   b. Warriors won

c. Series tied

d. Finals canceled

29. Which Warriors player was a significant factor in the playoff rivalry with the Mavericks in 2007 and beyond?

a. Stephen Curry

b. Klay Thompson

c. Kevin Durant

d. Baron Davis

30. In the 2015-2016 NBA season, the Mavericks faced the Oklahoma City Thunder in a playoff series. What was unique about this matchup?

a. It was the first playoff meeting between the teams

b. Dirk Nowitzki scored 50 points in a game

c. The series went to seven overtimes

d. Both teams set a record for three-pointers in a playoff game

ANSWERS

1. San Antonio Spurs

2. Texas Cup

3. 2001-2002

4. Clyde Drexler

5. Playoff brawl

6. Spurs won 4-3

7. Bruce Bowen

8. I-35

9. Oklahoma City Thunder

10. Dwyane Wade

11. Heat won

12. Jason Terry

13. 2011

14. Kevin Durant

15. Points Parade

16. Mavericks won

17. James Worthy

18. Showtime vs. Big D

19. It went to seven overtimes

20. Portland Trail Blazers

21. Gulf Coast Clash

22. 1994

23. Latrell Sprewell

24. Houston Rockets

25. 1985

26. Jazz Jump Ball

27. It was the first playoff meeting between the teams

28. Warriors won

29. Baron Davis

30. It was the first playoff meeting between the teams

COMMUNITY MANAGEMENT
QUESTION TIME!

1. What is the name of the Dallas Mavericks' community outreach program?

   a. Mavs Assist

   b. Mavericks Cares

   c. Hoops for Hope

   d. Dallas Gives Back

2. Which initiative focuses on encouraging children to read and learn through literacy programs by the Dallas Mavericks?

   a. Slam Dunk Reading

   b. Books and Baskets

   c. Mavs Literacy Program

   d. Read to Achieve

3. The Dallas Mavericks partner with local schools for various educational programs. What is the name of this initiative?

   a. School Slam

   b. Mavericks U

   c. Mavs Academy

   d. Classroom Mavericks

4. Which annual event brings together the Mavericks players, coaches, and staff to engage in community service projects?

    a. Mavs Volunteer Day

    b. Hoops for Humanity

    c. Mavericks Cares Day

    d. Community Slam Jam

5. The Mavericks host an annual "Seats for Soldiers" night, providing complimentary tickets to military personnel. In which month does this event typically take place?

    a. November

    b. December

    c. January

    d. February

6. What is the name of the program that supports underprivileged youth by providing them with the opportunity to attend Mavericks games?

    a. Mavs Scholars

    b. Courtside Kids

    c. Hoops for Hope

    d. Mavs Academy

7. The Mavericks collaborate with local organizations to address social issues. What is the name of this community-focused platform?

a. Mavericks Impact

b. Dallas Unite

c. Community Connect

d. Mavs Foundation

8. Which charitable foundation associated with the Mavericks aims to improve the lives of children, women, and families in need?

a. Mavs Care Foundation

b. Mavericks Charities

c. Dallas Gives Back Foundation

d. Hoops for Hope Foundation

9. The Mavericks support local youth basketball through various programs. What is the name of the youth basketball initiative?

a. Junior Mavs

b. Hoops for Kids

c. Youth Slam Dunk

d. Mavs Academy Youth League

10. What is the name of the annual event where the Mavericks players and staff serve Thanksgiving meals to those in need?

a. Mavs Turkey Drive

b. Hoops for Thanks

c. Giving Dunk Feast

d. Thanksgiving Slam Jam

11. The Mavericks host a yearly event where they recognize and honor outstanding community leaders. What is the name of this event?

a. Community All-Stars Awards

b. Mavericks Heroes Night

c. Mavs Impact Gala

d. Dallas Cares Recognition

12. Which program encourages physical fitness and healthy living among youth through basketball and other activities?

a. Fit Mavs

b. Hoops for Health

c. Active Mavericks

d. Health Slam Dunk

13. The Mavericks partner with local non-profits to address homelessness and provide support. What is the name of this initiative?

a. Shelter Slam

b. Home Court Hope

c. Hoops for Homes

d. Dallas Assistance Project

14. In collaboration with the NBA Cares initiative, the Mavericks participate in which program to promote social responsibility and community engagement?

a. NBA Impact

b. Hoops for Change

c. NBA Cares Hoops for Hope

d. Team Up for Change

15. Which initiative aims to create a positive impact on the community by addressing social justice issues and promoting equality?

a. Mavs Stand Up

b. Equality Slam

c. Mavericks for Justice

d. Hoops for Equality

16. The Mavericks organize an annual basketball camp for kids during the summer. What is the name of this camp?

   a. Mavs Hoop Camp

   b. Mavericks Summer Slam

   c. Hoops Adventure Camp

   d. Courtside Camp

17. What is the name of the mentoring program launched by the Mavericks that pairs team executives with local high school students?

   a. Mavericks Mentors

   b. Hoops for Leadership

   c. Dallas Futures

   d. Mavs Executive Mentorship

18. The Mavericks support military veterans through various programs. What is the name of their initiative dedicated to veterans?

   a. Hoops for Heroes

   b. Mavs Veterans Outreach

   c. Mavericks Salute

   d. Veterans Slam Dunk

19. The Mavericks collaborate with local businesses to provide job opportunities for young adults. What is the name of this workforce development initiative?

a. Mavs Jobs Connect

b. Hoops for Careers

c. Dallas Employment Project

d. Mavericks Career Hub

20. In collaboration with local law enforcement, the Mavericks host events to promote positive interactions between police and the community. What is the name of this initiative?

a. Hoops and Harmony

b. Unity Slam Jam

c. Mavs and Cops

d. Dallas Police Connect

21. The Mavericks host an annual event focused on celebrating diversity and inclusion. What is the name of this event?

a. Mavs Diversity Night

b. Unity Slam Fest

c. Hoops for Harmony

d. Dallas Diversity Gala

22. The Mavericks partner with local organizations to provide food assistance to those in need. What is the name of this community outreach effort?

a. Mavs Meals for All

b. Hoops for Hunger

c. Dallas Food Drive

d. Mavericks Cares Kitchen

23. What is the name of the program that provides financial literacy education to youth, empowering them with financial skills?

a. Mavs Financial Slam

b. Hoops for Finance

c. Mavericks Money Matters

d. Slam Dunk Finances

24. The Mavericks host an annual charity golf tournament to raise funds for community initiatives. What is the name of this tournament?

a. Mavs Golf Classic

b. Hoops on the Green

c. Mavericks Charity Open

d. Dallas Golf Slam

25. What is the name of the

initiative where Mavericks players and staff volunteer their time to renovate or build basketball courts in underserved communities?

a. Mavs Hoops Renovation

b. Courtside Care Project

c. Hoops for All Initiative

d. Mavericks Rebound Courts

26. The Mavericks collaborate with local artists for initiatives that promote art and creativity in the community. What is the name of this program?

a. Mavs Arts Slam

b. Hoops and Brushes

c. Artistic Mavericks

d. Dallas Canvas Project

27. The Mavericks participate in environmental sustainability efforts. What is the name of their initiative focused on green practices?

a. Mavs Green Slam

b. Hoops for Earth

c. Dallas Eco Slam

d. Mavericks Green Zone

28. What is the name of the program that provides scholarships and educational support to deserving students in the Dallas area?

a. Mavs Scholars

b. Hoops for Education

c. Mavericks Academic Excellence

d. Slam Dunk Scholarships

29. The Mavericks partner with local healthcare organizations for health and wellness initiatives. What is the name of this program?

a. Mavs Wellness Slam

b. Hoops for Health

c. Dallas Fitness Project

d. Mavericks Healthy Living

30. In which month do the Mavericks typically host their annual Fan Jam event, engaging with fans and the community?

a. September

b. October

c. November

d. December

ANSWERS

1. Mavericks Cares

2. Read to Achieve

3. Mavericks U

4. Mavericks Cares Day

5. December

6. Courtside Kids

7. Community Connect

8. Mavericks Charities

9. Junior Mavs

10. Mavs Turkey Drive

11. Mavs Impact Gala

12. Hoops for Health

13. Hoops for Homes

14. NBA Cares Hoops for Hope

15. Mavs Stand Up

16. Mavs Hoop Camp

17. Mavs Executive Mentorship

18. Hoops for Heroes

19. Mavs Jobs Connect

20. Mavs and Cops

21. Hoops for Harmony

22. Hoops for Hunger

23. Slam Dunk Finances

24. Mavs Golf Classic

25. Mavericks Rebound Courts

26. Mavs Arts Slam

27. Hoops for Earth

28. Mavs Scholars

29. Hoops for Health

30. November

TEAM MASCOT AND TRADITIONS
QUESTION TIME!

1. What is the name of the official mascot of the Dallas Mavericks?

   a. Mavs Man

   b. Dunkin' Dino

   c. Mavericks Max

   d. Hoop Hound

2. Which former Mavericks player served as the team's mascot for a brief period?

   a. Dirk Nowitzki

   b. Jason Terry

   c. Michael Finley

   d. Rolando Blackman

3. The Mavericks' mascot is known for entertaining fans with acrobatic dunks. What is the mascot's signature dunk called?

   a. Slammin' Maverick

   b. Mavs Dunk Fury

   c. Sky-High Slam

   d. Mania Dunk

4. What is the name of the tradition where the Mavericks celebrate the retirement of a player's jersey by raising it to the rafters?

a. Jersey Night

b. Mavericks Honor

c. Rafters Ceremony

d. Jersey Retirement

5. In which year did the Dallas Mavericks retire Dirk Nowitzki's jersey number?

a. 2018

b. 2019

c. 2020

d. 2021

6. What is the name of the special ceremony held in honor of Dirk Nowitzki's jersey retirement?

a. Dirk Tribute Night

b. Dirk Forever Celebration

c. Dirk's Last Dance

d. One Last Dirk

7. Which former Mavericks player had his jersey retired in 2003, becoming the first in franchise history?

a. Rolando Blackman

b. Derek Harper

c. Brad Davis

d. Mark Aguirre

8. The Mavericks have a tradition of playing a distinctive song during home games. What is the name of this song?

a. "Mavs Anthem"

b. "Dallas Beats"

c. "Go Mavs Go"

d. "The Horse"

9. Which traditional song is played when the Mavericks make a three-point shot during home games?

a. "Downtown Mavericks"

b. "Triple Threat Tune"

c. "Three-Point Symphony"

d. "Deep in the Heart of Texas"

10. The Dallas Mavericks have a tradition of a pregame light show accompanied by a specific song. What is the name of the song?

a. "Mavs Unleashed"

b. "Lights On"

c. "Mavs Ignition"

d. "Power Up"

11. Which former Mavericks player is known for starting the tradition of twirling a towel during games, inspiring fans to do the same?

a. Jason Kidd

b. Michael Finley

c. Derek Harper

d. Roy Tarpley

12. The Mavericks have a tradition of a halftime performance involving dancing horses. What is the name of this performance?

a. Mavericks Rodeo

b. Halftime Stampede

c. Buckin' Bronco Ballet

d. Horsepower Halftime

13. What is the name of the fan tradition where fans stand and cheer until the Mavericks make their first basket during a home game?

a. Mavs Roar

b. First Point Frenzy

c. Stand and Deliver

d. The Mavericks Challenge

14. The Mavericks introduced a tradition in 2019 where fans gather outside the arena to welcome the team. What is this tradition called?

a. Mavs March

b. Victory Walk

c. Dallas Arrival

d. Street Salute

15. During home games, the Mavericks feature a "Dance Cam" that focuses on fans dancing in the crowd. What is the name of the dance cam?

a. Mavs Groove Cam

b. Dance Fever Cam

c. Dallas Dance Off

d. Fan Moves Cam

16. What is the name of the tradition where the Dallas Mavericks honor military personnel during games?

a. Mavs Military Tribute

b. Armed Forces Salute

c. Hoops for Heroes

d. Military Mavericks Moment

17. The Dallas Mavericks have a tradition of recognizing a "Hero of the Game" during each home game. Who is typically honored with this title?

a. A fan with a heroic story

b. The leading scorer of the game

c. The head coach

d. The team owner

18. In 2019, the Mavericks introduced a tradition where a local musician performs the national anthem before home games. What is this tradition called?

a. Mavericks Anthem Series

b. National Anthem Jam

c. Dallas Star-Spangled Showcase

d. Anthem Spotlight

19. The Mavericks have a tradition of hosting theme nights during the season. What is the name of the annual theme night that celebrates international cultures?

a. Mavs Global Night

b. International Extravaganza

c. Global Heritage Night

d. Mavericks Around the World

20. What is the name of the tradition where fans receive a replica championship ring during a special promotional night?

a. Ring Night

b. Championship Bling

c. Replica Ring Giveaway

d. Mavs Ring Fling

21. The Mavericks have a tradition of engaging fans with interactive games on the arena's video boards. What is the name of this interactive experience?

a. Mavs Arcade

b. Hoops Interactive

c. Fan Games Zone

d. Big D Gaming

22. What is the name of the tradition where the Mavericks honor and celebrate local first responders during a home game?

a. Mavericks First Responders Night

b. Heroes Among Us

c. First Responder Salute

d. Mavs Brave Heroes

23. The Mavericks have a tradition of involving fans in selecting the "Fan of the Game." What is the criteria for being chosen as the Fan of the Game?

a. Best costume

b. Most enthusiastic fan

c. Longest consecutive game attendance

d. Random seat selection

24. In 2020, the Mavericks introduced a virtual fan experience for remote fans during games. What is the name of this initiative?

a. Mavs Virtual Fan Zone

b. Remote Row Mavericks

c. Fan Connection Hub

d. Dallas Virtual Crowd

25. What is the name of the tradition where the Mavericks celebrate and recognize their youngest fans during select home games?

a. Little Mavs Night

b. Kids Appreciation

c. Junior Mavericks Spotlight

d. Young Fan Extravaganza

26. The Mavericks have a tradition of presenting special giveaways to fans during certain promotional nights. What is the name of this initiative?

    a. Mavs Swag Night

    b. Dallas Giveaway Spectacular

    c. Fan Appreciation Giveback

    d. Mavs Freebies Frenzy

27. What is the name of the tradition where the Mavericks acknowledge and honor local teachers for their contributions?

    a. Teacher Tribute Night

    b. Educators Appreciation

    c. Mavs Teachers' Corner

    d. Teacher Excellence Awards

28. During home games, the Mavericks have a tradition of showcasing young talent from the local community. What is the name of this initiative?

    a. Mavs Youth Spotlight

    b. Dallas Rising Stars

    c. Future Mavericks Showcase

    d. Junior Jam Session

29. What is the name of the tradition where the Mavericks host a special night to celebrate and recognize their season ticket holders?

a. Mavs VIP Night

b. Season Ticket Holder Soiree

c. Dallas Mavericks Appreciation Night

d. Mavs Season Ticket Showcase

30. The Mavericks have a tradition of engaging fans in interactive contests during timeouts. What is the name of this entertaining tradition?

a. Mavs Timeout Showdown

b. Timeout Madness

c. Big D Break

d. Mavericks Timeout Spectacle

ANSWERS

1. a. Mavs Man

2. c. Michael Finley

3. d. Mania Dunk

4. d. Jersey Retirement

5. c. 2020

6. c. Dirk's Last Dance

7. a. Rolando Blackman

8. d. "The Horse"

9. d. "Deep in the Heart of Texas"

10. c. "Mavs Ignition"

11. b. Michael Finley

12. a. Mavericks Rodeo

13. d. The Mavericks Challenge

14. a. Mavs March

15. a. Mavs Groove Cam

16. c. Hoops for Heroes

17. a. A fan with a heroic story

18. a. Mavericks Anthem Series

19. c. Global Heritage Night

20. d. Mavs Ring Fling

21. a. Mavs Arcade

22. a. Mavericks First Responders Night

23. d. Random seat selection

24. d. Dallas Virtual Crowd

25. a. Little Mavs Night

26. c. Fan Appreciation Giveback

27. a. Teacher Tribute Night

28. c. Future Mavericks Showcase

29. b. Season Ticket Holder Soiree

30. a. Mavs Timeout Showdown

JERSEY HISTORY DESIGN
QUESTION TIME!

1. What are the primary team colors of the Dallas Mavericks?

   a. Blue and Green

   b. Navy Blue and White

   c. Royal Blue and Silver

   d. Red and Black

2. In which year did the Dallas Mavericks unveil their inaugural team jerseys?

   a. 1978

   b. 1980

   c. 1982

   d. 1985

3. The Mavericks' original jerseys featured a prominent logo on the shorts. What was the design of this logo?

   a. Texas flag

   b. Cowboy hat

   c. Basketball

   d. Maverick horse

4. During the early years, the Mavericks had a distinctive design element on their jerseys. What was it?

a. Pinstripes

b. Checkered pattern

c. Gradient color

d. Zigzag stripes

5. The Mavericks introduced a new jersey design in the 2001-2002 season, coinciding with a rebranding effort. What significant change was made to the jerseys?

a. Addition of a secondary logo

b. Introduction of a new font for player names

c. Change in team colors

d. Incorporation of a side panel design

6. In 2001, the Mavericks introduced a green alternate jersey. What was the inspiration behind this unique design?

a. St. Patrick's Day

b. Environmental awareness

c. Tribute to the Dallas Stars

d. Irish heritage

7. The Mavericks' jerseys underwent a significant redesign in 2017. What was the primary focus of this redesign?

a. Simplification of the overall design

b. Introduction of a new team mascot logo

c. Incorporation of a futuristic theme

d. Tribute to the team's history

8. The current Dallas Mavericks jerseys feature the team's wordmark across the chest. What font is used for the wordmark?

a. Arial

b. Impact

c. Helvetica

d. Futura

9. The Mavericks occasionally wear special "City Edition" jerseys. What was the theme of the City Edition jerseys in the 2020-2021 season?

a. Neon Lights

b. Texas Heritage

c. Skyline Tribute

d. Retro Revival

10. The Mavericks collaborated with a famous streetwear designer for the "City Edition" jerseys in the 2021-2022 season. Who was the designer?

a. Virgil Abloh

b. Don C

c. Jerry Lorenzo

d. Jeff Staple

11. The Dallas Mavericks have worn throwback jerseys to honor their early years. What era do these throwback jerseys typically represent?

a. 1980s

b. 1990s

c. 2000s

d. 2010s

12. In the 1990s, the Mavericks introduced a jersey with a logo featuring a horse dribbling a basketball. What was the nickname given to this logo?

a. Maverick Stallion

b. Dribble Horse

c. Hoop Hound

d. Bucking Bronco

13. The Mavericks' skyline-themed jerseys pay homage to the city of Dallas. Which iconic building is often featured in the skyline design?

a. Reunion Tower

b. Bank of America Plaza

c. Fountain Place

d. Omni Dallas Hotel

14. The Mavericks' jerseys have featured various jersey sponsors over the years. Which company became the team's jersey sponsor in the 2017-2018 season?

a. American Airlines

b. AT&T

c. 7-Eleven

d. Dr Pepper

15. The Mavericks celebrated their 40th season in the NBA with a special jersey patch. What design element was incorporated into this anniversary patch?

a. A basketball with the number 40

b. A stylized Mavericks logo

c. The Dallas skyline

d. A tribute to the original team colors

16. The Dallas Mavericks have occasionally worn jerseys with Spanish-themed designs to celebrate Noche Latina. What does "Noche Latina" translate to in English?

a. Latin Night

b. Night of Stars

c. Spanish Heritage Night

d. Latino Celebration

17. In the 1980s, the Mavericks had a unique jersey design that featured a colorful gradient pattern. What were the primary colors of this gradient?

a. Blue and Green

b. Red and Yellow

c. Purple and Orange

d. Black and Gray

18. The Mavericks' "Hardwood Classics" jerseys pay homage to the team's early years. What specific design element is featured on these throwback jerseys?

a. Pinstripes

b. Checkered pattern

c. Zigzag stripes

d. Gradient color

19. The Mavericks' jerseys often feature a small Texas flag patch. Where is this patch typically located on the jersey?

a. Above the team logo

b. On the back collar

c. On the shorts

d. Next to the player's name

20. The Dallas Mavericks' original home jerseys had a distinctive design on the shorts that resembled:

a. A basketball court

b. A cowboy hat

c. A pair of basketball shoes

d. A horseshoe

21. What material is commonly used for the lettering and numbering on the Mavericks' jerseys?

a. Felt

b. Twill

c. Leather

d. Silk

22. The Mavericks' "Association" jerseys typically feature which primary color?

a. Blue

b. White

c. Silver

d. Green

23. The Mavericks' "Icon" jerseys are often worn for home games and feature which primary color?

a. Blue

b. White

c. Silver

d. Green

24. The Mavericks introduced a "Statement" jersey as part of the Nike NBA uniform system. What is the primary characteristic of the "Statement" jerseys?

a. Bold color accents

b. Subdued and minimalist design

c. Camouflage pattern

d. Retro styling

25. The Mavericks' jerseys have undergone changes in font styles over the years. Which font style is associated with the Mavericks' classic jerseys from the 1980s?

a. Serif

b. Script

c. Sans-serif

d. Gothic

26. The Mavericks celebrated their 30th season with a special jersey patch. What design element was featured on this anniversary patch?

a. A basketball with the number 30

b. A commemorative logo

c. The Mavericks' championship trophy

d. The number 30 in Roman numerals

27. In the 2018-2019 season, the Mavericks introduced a "City Edition" jersey inspired by:

a. The Texas flag

b. The Dallas skyline

c. The team's original logo

d. The state flower

28. The Mavericks' jerseys have a unique neckline

design. What is the style of the neckline commonly seen on the team's jerseys?

a. V-neck

b. Crew neck

c. Scoop neck

d. Henley neck

29. The Mavericks' "Earned Edition" jerseys are typically worn by teams that:

a. Have the best records in the previous season

b. Win an NBA Championship

c. Achieve a significant milestone

d. Receive special fan votes

30. The Mavericks' jerseys often have a jock tag featuring the team's logo and other details. Where is this jock tag typically located on the jersey?

a. Near the waistline

b. On the back collar

c. On the sleeves

d. Next to the player's name

ANSWERS

1. c. Royal Blue and Silver

2. a. 1978

3. a. Texas flag

4. a. Pinstripes

5. d. Incorporation of a side panel design

6. a. St. Patrick's Day

7. a. Simplification of the overall design

8. d. Futura

9. c. Skyline Tribute

10. b. Don C

11. a. 1980s

12. c. Hoop Hound

13. a. Reunion Tower

14. b. AT&T

15. a. A basketball with the number 40

16. a. Latin Night

17. c. Purple and Orange

18. a. Pinstripes

19. c. On the shorts

20. b. A cowboy hat

21. b. Twill

22. a. Blue

23. b. White

24. a. Bold color accents

25. b. Script

26. a. A basketball with the number 30

27. b. The Dallas skyline

28. c. Scoop neck

29. a. Have the best records in the previous season

30. a. Near the waistline

FAN BASE
QUESTION TIME!

1. What is the nickname commonly used for Dallas Mavericks fans?

   a. Mavs Nation

   b. Mavericks Maniacs

   c. Mavs Crew

   d. Dallas Fanatics

2. The Dallas Mavericks have a dedicated fan club for young fans. What is the name of this fan club?

   a. Mavs Youth Squad

   b. Junior Mavs

   c. Little Mavericks Club

   d. Mavs Junior Nation

3. The Mavericks' fan base is known for a unique tradition during games. What do fans often do when the opposing team shoots free throws?

   a. Stand silently

   b. Wave foam fingers

   c. Bang thundersticks

   d. Engage in coordinated chants

4. What is the name of the Mavericks' official fan engagement platform where fans can connect and interact with the team?

a. Mavs Fan Hub

b. Mavericks Connect

c. Dallas Fan Zone

d. MFFL Community

5. The term "MFFL" is commonly associated with Dallas Mavericks fans. What does "MFFL" stand for?

a. Mavericks Fan For Life

b. Mavs Forever Love

c. Mavericks Faithful for Life

d. Mavs Fanatic Living

6. What is the iconic gesture often seen among Mavericks fans, inspired by a former player's celebration?

a. The Dirk Wave

b. The Jet Point

c. The Kidd Clap

d. The Finley Jump

7. Mavericks fans are known for their passionate support during games. What is the nickname given to the loud and enthusiastic fans?

a. Mavericks Roar

b. Mavs Maniacs

c. Dallas Thunder

d. MFFL Crew

8. The Dallas Mavericks host an annual event where fans can meet players and enjoy various activities. What is the name of this fan-focused event?

a. Mavs Fest

b. Fan Jam

c. Dallas Fan Fest

d. MFFL Day

9. Which social media platform is particularly popular among Mavericks fans for sharing their passion and connecting with the team?

a. Twitter

b. Instagram

c. Facebook

d. TikTok

10. What is the traditional saying or chant that Mavericks fans often use to express their loyalty to the team?

a. "Mavs for Life!"

b. "Go Mavs Go!"

c. "Dallas Forever!"

d. "MFFL Pride!"

11. Mavericks fans often wear a specific color to create a coordinated look during home games. What is this designated color?

a. Blue

b. White

c. Green

d. Silver

12. The Dallas Mavericks launched a fan loyalty program. What is the name of this program that rewards fans for their continuous support?

a. Mavs Loyalty Club

b. MFFL Rewards

c. Mavericks FanZone

d. Dallas Loyalty Program

13. Mavericks fans have a special gesture for showing appreciation to players. What is this gesture that involves holding up three fingers?

  a. The Dirk Salute

  b. The Three-Point Wave

  c. The Mavericks Signal

  d. The Triple Cheers

14. In 2019, the Mavericks hosted an event where fans set a world record for the largest gathering of people dressed as superheroes. What was the theme of this event?

  a. Mavs Superhero Day

  b. Dallas Heroes Night

  c. MFFL Superpower Bash

  d. Mavericks Marvel Madness

15. The Dallas Mavericks have a fan council that provides feedback and insights to the team. What is the name of this fan advisory group?

  a. Mavs Voice

  b. Fan Feedback Council

  c. Mavericks Advisory Crew

  d. Dallas Fan Alliance

16. What is the name of the official podcast created for Mavericks fans, providing behind-the-scenes insights and interviews?

    a. Mavs Insider

    b. Dallas Hoops Talk

    c. MFFL Podcast

    d. Mavericks Unplugged

17. Mavericks fans are known for their creativity in designing signs and banners for games. What is the designated area in the arena where fans showcase their signs?

    a. Banner Boulevard

    b. Sign City

    c. Mavs Message Zone

    d. Fan Banner Row

18. During the playoffs, Mavericks fans often participate in a coordinated theme for home games. What is an example of a common playoff theme among fans?

    a. Blue Out

    b. White Out

    c. Green Out

    d. Silver Out

19. The Dallas Mavericks have a dedicated section in the arena where fans can enjoy premium experiences and perks. What is the name of this exclusive fan zone?

a. Mavs VIP Lounge

b. Mavericks Elite Zone

c. Dallas Fan Club

d. MFFL Premium

20. Mavericks fans express their opinions and engage in discussions on various online forums. What is one popular online platform for Mavericks fan discussions?

a. MavsTalk

b. DallasHoopsForum

c. MFFL Chat

d. Mavericks Fan Zone

21. In 2020, the Mavericks honored a longtime season ticket holder by featuring their image on the court. What is the name of this fan recognition initiative?

a. Fan of the Year Tribute

b. MFFL Hall of Fame

c. Season Ticket Holder Spotlight

d. Mavericks Superfan Showcase

22. The Dallas Mavericks celebrate Fan Appreciation Night each season. What special activities and giveaways are typically part of this event?

a. Exclusive merchandise discounts

b. Autographed memorabilia giveaways

c. Fan photo opportunities

d. All of the above

23. The Mavericks' official website features a fan zone with exclusive content and interactive experiences. What is the name of this online hub for Mavericks fans?

a. Mavs Connect

b. Fan Central

c. Dallas Mavericks Zone

d. MFFL Hub

24. Mavericks fans have a signature hand gesture that involves making a gesture with the hand while shouting "Let's Go Mavs!" What is this gesture?

a. Fist Pump

b. Peace Sign

c. Three-Finger Point

d. The Mavs Clap

25. What is the name of the charity initiative where Mavericks players and fans collaborate to support local communities?

a. Mavs Community Assist

b. Dallas Cares Together

c. Mavericks Helping Hands

d. MFFL Gives Back

26. The Dallas Mavericks have a fan engagement app that provides exclusive content and experiences. What is the name of this official app for Mavericks fans?

a. MFFL Experience

b. Mavs Fan Zone App

c. Dallas Mavericks Connect

d. Mavs Fanatics App

27. The Mavericks' fan base extends beyond the local community, with fans around the world. What is the name of the official global fan community for international Mavericks fans?

a. MFFL Global

b.

Mavericks Worldwide

c. Dallas Hoops International

d. Global Mavs Nation

28. Mavericks fans often participate in charity events and community service projects. What is the name of the annual initiative that encourages fans to volunteer and give back?

a. MFFL Cares Week

b. Mavericks Service Day

c. Dallas Volunteer Challenge

d. Fan Community Impact

29. The Dallas Mavericks host an annual event where fans can showcase their basketball skills and win prizes. What is the name of this fan-centric basketball tournament?

a. Mavs Hoops Challenge

b. Fan Jam Dunk Contest

c. Dallas Mavericks Skills Showcase

d. MFFL Hoops Invitational

30. Mavericks fans are known for their dedication and loyalty. What is the official tagline that reflects the bond between the team and its fans?

a. MFFL Unity

b. Mavericks Strong

c. Dallas Forever

d. Mavs Family

ANSWERS

1. a. Mavs Nation

2. b. Junior Mavs

3. c. Bang thundersticks

4. d. MFFL Community

5. c. Mavericks Faithful for Life

6. b. The Jet Point

7. b. Mavs Maniacs

8. b. Fan Jam

9. b. Instagram

10. b. "Go Mavs Go!"

11. b. White

12. b. MFFL Rewards

13. a. The Dirk Salute

14. a. Mavs Superhero Day

15. a. Mavs Voice

16. a. Mavs Insider

17. c. Mavs Message Zone

18. d. Silver Out

19. a. Mavs VIP Lounge

20. a. MavsTalk

21. c. Season Ticket Holder Spotlight

22. d. All of the above

23. b. Fan Central

24. c. Three-Finger Point

25. a. Mavs Community Assist

26. b. Mavs Fan Zone App

27. b. Mavericks Worldwide

28. b. Mavericks Service Day

29. a. Mavs Hoops Challenge

30. d. Mavs Family

COACHING STAFF
QUESTION TIME!

1. Who is the head coach of the Dallas Mavericks as of the latest information available?

   a. Rick Carlisle

   b. Jason Kidd

   c. Don Nelson

   d. Avery Johnson

2. Before becoming the head coach, Jason Kidd had a successful playing career. What position did he play during his NBA career?

   a. Shooting guard

   b. Small forward

   c. Point guard

   d. Power forward

3. Which former NBA team did Jason Kidd coach before joining the Dallas Mavericks?

   a. Brooklyn Nets

   b. Milwaukee Bucks

   c. Los Angeles Lakers

   d. Phoenix Suns

4. In which year did Jason Kidd become the head coach of the Dallas Mavericks?

a. 2018

b. 2019

c. 2020

d. 2021

5. Who is the associate head coach of the Dallas Mavericks, working closely with Jason Kidd?

a. Jamahl Mosley

b. Stephen Silas

c. Darrell Armstrong

d. Mike Shedd

6. Jamahl Mosley served as the interim head coach for the Dallas Mavericks in the past. During which season did he take on this role?

a. 2018-2019

b. 2019-2020

c. 2020-2021

d. 2021-2022

7. Before joining the Dallas Mavericks, Jamahl Mosley was an assistant coach for which NBA team?

a. Cleveland Cavaliers

b. Orlando Magic

c. Atlanta Hawks

d. Toronto Raptors

8. Who is the assistant coach responsible for player development on the Dallas Mavericks coaching staff?

a. Jenny Boucek

b. Darrell Armstrong

c. Stephen Silas

d. Mike Shedd

9. Darrell Armstrong, an assistant coach for the Mavericks, had a playing career in the NBA. What position did he primarily play?

a. Point guard

b. Shooting guard

c. Small forward

d. Power forward

10. Jenny Boucek joined the Dallas Mavericks as an assistant coach, making history as the first full-time female coach in franchise history. What is her specific role?

    a. Offensive coordinator

    b. Defensive coordinator

    c. Player development

    d. Head of scouting

11. Before joining the Mavericks, Jenny Boucek worked with which NBA team's coaching staff?

    a. Sacramento Kings

    b. Los Angeles Lakers

    c. Golden State Warriors

    d. Houston Rockets

12. Who is the special assistant to the head coach for the Dallas Mavericks, providing support to Jason Kidd?

    a. Devin Harris

    b. Dirk Nowitzki

    c. Michael Finley

    d. Tyson Chandler

13. Devin Harris, a former NBA player, serves in a coaching role for the Mavericks. What is his specific title?

a. Assistant coach

b. Player development coach

c. Special advisor

d. Director of basketball operations

14. Michael Finley is involved in the Mavericks' front office but also contributes to coaching decisions. What is his official title?

a. Vice President of Basketball Operations

b. Director of Scouting

c. Assistant General Manager

d. Chief Executive Officer

15. Who is the director of basketball operations for the Dallas Mavericks, overseeing various aspects of the team's basketball activities?

a. Keith Grant

b. J.J. Barea

c. Donnie Nelson

d. Michael Finley

16. Before becoming involved in coaching and front-office roles, J.J. Barea had a successful playing career with the Mavericks. What position did he play?

a. Point guard

b. Shooting guard

c. Small forward

d. Power forward

17. J.J. Barea serves as the director of basketball operations but also has a role as a player mentor. What does this role involve?

a. Providing financial advice to players

b. Mentoring young players on and off the court

c. Organizing team events

d. Managing player contracts

18. Who is the vice president of basketball operations for the Dallas Mavericks, responsible for overseeing the team's overall basketball strategy?

a. Donnie Nelson

b. Mark Cuban

c. Jason Kidd

d. Michael Finley

19. Donnie Nelson, a key figure in the Mavericks' front office, is also the general manager of the team. True or False?

20. Which former NBA player serves as a player development coach for the Dallas Mavericks, focusing on improving the skills of individual players?

a. Darrell Armstrong

b. God Shammgod

c. Mike Shedd

d. Jenny Boucek

21. God Shammgod, known for his unique dribbling technique, is part of the Mavericks coaching staff. What is his specific role?

a. Shooting coach

b. Dribbling specialist

c. Defensive coordinator

d. Offensive strategist

22. Mike Shedd, an assistant coach for the Mavericks, specializes in coaching which area of the game?

a. Shooting

b. Defense

c. Rebounding

d. Player conditioning

23. Which former NBA player serves as the player development coach for the Dallas Mavericks, working on enhancing the skills of the team's big men?

    a. Tyson Chandler

    b. Dirk Nowitzki

    c. Shawn Bradley

    d. Erick Dampier

24. Tyson Chandler, a former NBA champion with the Mavericks, serves in a coaching role. What is his specific title?

    a. Defensive coordinator

    b. Player development coach

    c. Special advisor

    d. Offensive strategist

25. Which coach on the Mavericks staff has a role specifically focused on the team's offensive strategies and plays?

    a. Stephen Silas

    b. Darrell Armstrong

    c. Mike Shedd

    d. Jenny Boucek

26. Who is responsible for overseeing the Mavericks' defensive strategies and player rotations as an assistant coach?

a. Jamahl Mosley

b. Stephen Silas

c. Mike Shedd

d. God Shammgod

27. Stephen Silas, before joining the Mavericks, had coaching experience with which NBA team?

a. Golden State Warriors

b. Houston Rockets

c. Los Angeles Clippers

d. Chicago Bulls

28. Who is the shooting coach for the Dallas Mavericks, focusing on improving the shooting skills of the players?

a. Mike Shedd

b. God Shammgod

c. Darrell Armstrong

d. Peter Patton

29. Peter Patton, a shooting coach for the Mavericks, has a background in coaching which sport before joining the NBA?

a. Basketball

b. Soccer

c. Baseball

d. Tennis

30. Which coach on the Mavericks staff has a role specifically focused on strength and conditioning, ensuring players are in optimal physical condition?

a. Mike Shedd

b. God Shammgod

c. Darrell Armstrong

d. Casey Smith

ANSWERS

1. b. Jason Kidd

2. c. Point guard

3. a. Brooklyn Nets

4. c. 2020

5. a. Jamahl Mosley

6. c. 2020-2021

7. b. Orlando Magic

8. a. Jenny Boucek

9. a. Point guard

10. c. Player development

11. a. Sacramento Kings

12. a. Devin Harris

13. a. Assistant coach

14. a. Vice President of Basketball Operations

15. a. Keith Grant

16. a. Point guard

17. b. Mentoring young players on and off the court

18. a. Donnie Nelson

19. False

20. b. God Shammgod

21. b. Dribbling specialist

22. a. Shooting

23. a. Tyson Chandler

24. c. Special advisor

25. d. Jenny Boucek

26. a. Jamahl Mosley

27. b. Houston Rockets

28. d. Peter Patton

29. b. Soccer

30. d. Casey Smith

Made in the USA
Coppell, TX
12 December 2024

42328085R00069